Helen's Special Picture

A Children's Story about

Sister Faustina

Written and Illustrated by
David Previtali

Marian Press
Marians of the Immaculate Conception
Stockbridge, Massachusetts

2000

Pope John Paul II canonized St. Faustina
in Rome on April 30, 2000,
Divine Mercy Sunday.
The 1st Saint of the new Millenium.

Available from: Marian Helpers Center, Stockbridge, MA 01263
Prayer Line: 1-800-804-3823 • Orderline: 1-800-462-7426 • Website: www.marian.org

ISBN 0-944203-42-6

Editing and Proofreading by David Came, Stephen LaChance, and Mary Ellen McDonald

Typesetting and Design by Bill Sosa and Paula Hegarty

Cover Design by Mitch Kruszyna
based on an illustration of Sister Faustina by David R. Previtali

Illustrations throughout text by David R. Previtali

Printed in the United States of America by the Marian Press,
Stockbridge, Massachusetts 01263

To Marian,
my wife of 18 years,
with all my love.

Not very long ago, in the land of Poland, there lived a little girl named Helen. She was a lovely girl with beautiful gray eyes and strawberry blond hair, which she wore in long braids.

Helen lived in a small village. Her Daddy was a farmer and a carpenter, and she had two brothers and seven sisters. Their family was poor, but not as poor as some of their neighbors.

Helen had a very generous and loving heart. She used to feel sorry for people or animals who were sick or suffering. She tried to help them in many ways. Whenever the poor came to her door, she always found something to give them.

Once, when she was ten years old, Helen thought up a secret plan to help the poor. She put on patched, ragged clothes, looking quite like an old beggar woman. Then she went around the village collecting money.

Another time Helen held a raffle. She asked her friends for little gifts to use as prizes, and she sold tickets for a penny a piece. Almost everyone she asked in the village bought a ticket!

Helen took the little money she had collected to her parish priest. She asked him to give it to the poor. How happy they were to have some money to buy food and clothing!

One of the happiest times in Helen's life was the day of her First Holy Communion. All the girls were so excited about getting new dresses, and carrying candles with bouquets of flowers.

Helen loved new dresses and flowers, too. But she was more excited about receiving Jesus in the Eucharist. She couldn't imagine anything better than that!

After the First Communion Mass, the girls were asked what they had liked best. Some said that their fancy dresses were best. Others thought it was the colorful flowers which decorated the church.

But Helen had the smartest answer. She said, "The best thing was Jesus coming to me in Holy Communion."

helen was a very good storyteller. Her friends used to beg her to tell them stories from the Bible.

They would sit under the shade of a large tree in the garden, listening to stories about Noah, or Moses, or about Joseph and his coat of many colors.

Helen also told them stories about Jesus, the Son of God and our Savior. Their eyes grew wide with wonder as they heard how Saint Joseph and Mary traveled to Bethlehem, and how the little Lord Jesus was born in a dark stable among the cows and sheep.

12

They clapped their hands with excitement as Helen spoke of the many miracles of Jesus, like changing water into wine, calming a terrible storm at sea, or curing the sick!

Sometimes they cried when she told them how Jesus was arrested and died on the cross to take away our sin.

But their sorrow turned to joy when they remembered that He rose up from the dead on the first Easter Sunday!

When Helen was a teenager, she got a job to help earn money for her family. She became a maid for the village baker.

Her days were spent cooking delicious meals, doing the laundry, and cleaning house. It was a lot of work, but she never complained. She tried to do everything with a smile!

Helen loved to pray and to sing religious songs. Her favorite prayer was the rosary, which her family always said together every night at home. Many times she would get up in the middle of the night, turn towards the parish church, and pray to Jesus in the Blessed Sacrament.

As Helen grew older, she began to think of what God wanted her to do with her life. When she was twenty years old, she decided that God wanted her to become a nun. She would spend her whole life serving others as Jesus did!

Helen joined a community of nuns called the Sisters of Our Lady of Mercy. These Sisters served God by trying to help girls who had gotten into trouble.

Helen was now called Sister Faustina. She was very happy to be one of Jesus' special followers. She was so glad to be a nun!

One day, not long after she became a nun, something wonderful happened to Sister Faustina.

Jesus came down from Heaven and appeared to her! He told her that she was to be His special messenger and helper.

She was to remind everyone about the Good News of God's mercy. Mercy means that God loves us and forgives us our sins. He wants us to live forever with Him in Heaven!

Jesus asked Sister Faustina to have a special picture made of Him! He told her that it would help many people to trust in His mercy.

20

The picture showed Jesus dressed in a long white robe.

His right hand was raised in blessing. His left hand was resting upon His chest. From His chest, two dazzling rays shone forth.

One ray was red. It was a reminder that Jesus shed His blood for us upon the cross. The other was pale, very much like the color of water. It stood for the Sacrament of Baptism which makes us children of God.

At the bottom of the picture were the words, "Jesus, I Trust In You!"

At first, no one knew that Jesus had appeared to Sister Faustina. It was a secret she shared only with the priest who heard her confessions. He agreed to help her do all that Jesus asked.

They found an artist to paint the picture of Jesus. Sister Faustina was so disappointed when she saw the finished picture. Jesus didn't look as beautiful as she had seen Him. But Our Lord told her that it didn't matter. What mattered was that people trust in Him and honor the picture in their churches and homes.

Holy cards of the picture were given to others. Sometimes God worked miracles for those who prayed before the picture of Jesus, our Merciful Savior!

Sister Faustina was very glad that people were honoring Jesus painted in the special picture. Nothing made her happier than to see others trusting in Jesus!

Jesus appeared to her other times, too. He asked her to do many things. She wrote about all these things in her diary.

One time, Jesus taught her to pray a special prayer on her rosary beads called the chaplet of mercy. It is a prayer asking God to forgive the sins of the world.

Another time, He asked her to celebrate a special feast day called Mercy Sunday. On this day, people were to honor Jesus painted in the picture and to receive Him in Holy Communion.

Even though Jesus had chosen Sister Faustina to be His special helper, she didn't think that she was better than other people.

She lived like all the other Sisters, going to Mass every day and offering many prayers to God. Sometimes, she worked as a cook for the Sisters and the girls they helped. Other times, she cleaned house or took care of the garden.

When she was assigned to help the doorkeeper of the Sisters' house, Sister Faustina would help the poor who came asking for food. She loved and served them with all her heart.

She was happy to do whatever needed to be done, and she did everything with a smile. Wherever she went, she taught others to love and trust in Jesus, our Merciful Savior.

One day Sister Faustina became very sick. She had to spend a long time in the hospital where doctors tried to cure her illness. But she didn't get better. Instead, her sickness became worse. She knew it was time for her to go to Heaven soon.

Some Sisters who felt she was a special friend of Jesus, asked Sister Faustina to pray for them once she got to Heaven. That day came October 5, 1938. Sister Faustina was only thirty-three years old when she died. That's how old Jesus was when He died on the cross.

The other Sisters were very sad when Sister Faustina died. But when their prayers to her were answered, their sadness was turned into joy, for they knew that their dear friend was now with Jesus.

Sister Faustina has become very famous. Many people have heard about her mission as Jesus' special helper in sharing His mercy. They try to do all that Jesus asked of her.

They honor the picture of our Merciful Savior by giving it a special place in their homes. They pray the chaplet of mercy and celebrate Mercy Sunday to thank God for His great love for us. They try to be merciful like Jesus, helping others and living good Christian lives.

The Pope knows about Sister Faustina, too. He will soon declare her to be a Saint! The whole world is now learning about the story of Helen and her special picture. What a happy time this is for the Merciful Savior and Sister Faustina!

THE YOUNG LIFE OF
SISTER FAUSTINA
BY CLAIRE JORDAN MOHAN

The fascinating story of the life of Sr. Faustina is sure to captivate middle-school age readers. Start your young loved ones on a path of devotion to Our Merciful Lord and His "Apostle and Secretary of Divine Mercy."

"It held my attention all the way through!"
> — 12-year-old Andrea Wasuk, Lenox, MA

"It was a delight to read the moving story of Sister Faustina — special in her calling, special in her response, and special in her mission of Mercy."
> — Fr. George W. Kosicki, CSB, Author and Speaker on Divine Mercy

109 pages, 18 b/w illustrations
$7.95

Call toll-free **1-800-462-7426** to order (code **YLSF**).

Ask about postage and handling and method of shipment when you call.

MARIAN PRESS